the NLT
BIBLE
PROMISE
BOOK

for tough times

Tyndale House Publishers, Inc., Carol Stream, Illinois

Visit Tyndale online at www.tyndale.com.

TYNDALE, New Living Translation, NLT, the New Living Translation logo, and Tyndale's quill logo are registered trademarks of Tyndale House Publishers, Inc.

The NLT Bible Promise Book for Tough Times

Copyright © 2011 by Ronald A. Beers. All rights reserved.

Cover photo copyright © by Fancy/Veer. All rights reserved.

Designed by Jennifer Ghionzoli and Ruth Berg

Compiled and edited by Amy E. Mason. All rights reserved.

Scripture quotations are taken from the *Holy Bible*, New Living Translation, copyright © 1996, 2004, 2007 by Tyndale House Foundation. Used by permission of Tyndale House Publishers, Inc., Carol Stream, Illinois 60188. All rights reserved.

ISBN 978-1-4143-1235-4

Printed in China

❧ CONTENTS ❧

It might surprise you to hear that the Bible promises us that tough times will come. As long as we live in a sinful world, troubles will be part of our human experience. So what can we do? Just deal with it? grin and bear it? put a smile on our faces and pretend to ignore the pain? Or perhaps do the opposite and wallow in self-pity?

Along with the Bible's promise that tough times will come, God's Word also promises that there is present help and future hope as we live with pain and adversity. In every trouble, there is potential triumph. In every pain, we can find the very power of God to combat it. In all our suffering, we can find salvation, both in this life and for the next.

There is no better place than God's Word to discover this help and hope that we so desperately need. Isaiah 40:8 says, "The grass withers and the flowers fade, but the word of our God stands forever." This means we can trust that when God promises hope to those who believe in him, this hope will not end in disappointment. When God promises to comfort those who mourn, comfort will be supplied in perfect measure. When

God assures us that he loves us and that he has plans for our lives, we can know he is telling the truth. God is truth, and his Word has stood the tests of time and will continue to be trustworthy throughout eternity. So whatever you're going through, no matter your problems, you have God's forever promises to cling to while you're facing life's trials.

This book may be small in size, but it carries with it the powerful, eternal vows that God speaks to his people. These promises were delivered to people in other times who were struggling, but they were also meant for you. God's promises in this book are arranged in alphabetical order by topic, so they are easy to find. And you will find over three hundred of them here. Can you imagine anyone who can make that many promises and keep them perfectly? God can and does. He is always faithful to carry out his plans and to fulfill his promises.

As you read God's promises for tough times, picture God speaking directly to you. You will be amazed at how personal and deeply compassionate our God is. Our desire is that you will find new hope, be encouraged, and find rest in God's almighty presence in your life. Even when it feels as if the world you know is changing, you can feel secure in the arms of your everlasting God, the Alpha and the Omega, who was, is, and is to come. May God bless you for seeking him in your troubled times, and may you find that God is indeed with you always.

〰◌〰

ABANDONMENT

When you feel as if God has left you . . .

Those who know your name trust in you, for you, O LORD,
do not abandon those who search for you.
  Psalm 9:10

ABUSE

When you've been harmed . . .

We are hunted down, but never abandoned by God. We get
knocked down, but we are not destroyed.
  2 Corinthians 4:9

When you wonder if God understands your pain . . .

It was our weaknesses he carried; it was our sorrows that
weighed him down. And we thought his troubles were a
punishment from God, a punishment for his own sins! But
he was pierced for our rebellion, crushed for our sins. He was
beaten so we could be whole. He was whipped so we could
be healed.
Isaiah 53:4-5

When healing seems impossible . . .

He heals the brokenhearted and bandages their wounds.
Psalm 147:3

For you who fear my name, the Sun of Righteousness will rise
with healing in his wings. And you will go free, leaping with
joy like calves let out to pasture.
Malachi 4:2

A vast crowd brought to him people who were lame, blind,
crippled, those who couldn't speak, and many others. They
laid them before Jesus, and he healed them all.
Matthew 15:30

ACCUSATIONS

When you've been falsely accused . . .

Be careful to live properly among your unbelieving neighbors.
Then even if they accuse you of doing wrong, they will see
your honorable behavior, and they will give honor to God
when he judges the world.
1 Peter 2:12

Even if you suffer for doing what is right, God will reward you for it. So don't worry or be afraid of their threats.
1 Peter 3:14

Keep your conscience clear. Then if people speak against you, they will be ashamed when they see what a good life you live because you belong to Christ.
1 Peter 3:16

When you've jumped to false conclusions about someone else . . .

Don't make judgments about anyone ahead of time—before the Lord returns. For he will bring our darkest secrets to light and will reveal our private motives. Then God will give to each one whatever praise is due.
1 Corinthians 4:5

Make allowance for each other's faults, and forgive anyone who offends you. Remember, the Lord forgave you, so you must forgive others.
Colossians 3:13

ADDICTION

When you've lost all control . . .

Do not let sin control the way you live; do not give in to sinful desires. Do not let any part of your body become an instrument of evil to serve sin. Instead, give yourselves completely to God, for you were dead, but now you have new life. So use your whole body as an instrument to do what is right for the glory of God. Sin is no longer your master, for you no longer live under the requirements of the law. Instead, you live under the freedom of God's grace.

Romans 6:12-14

Letting your sinful nature control your mind leads to death. But letting the Spirit control your mind leads to life and peace.

Romans 8:6

When you doubt that God can free you from your sinful habits . . .

He sent out his word and healed them, snatching them from the door of death. Let them praise the Lord for his great love and for the wonderful things he has done for them.

Psalm 107:20-21

If the Son sets you free, you are truly free.

John 8:36

Because you belong to him, the power of the life-giving Spirit has freed you from the power of sin that leads to death.

Romans 8:2

The Holy Spirit produces this kind of fruit in our lives: love, joy, peace, patience, kindness, goodness, faithfulness, gentleness, and self-control. There is no law against these things!

Galatians 5:22-23

When someone you love struggles with addiction . . .

[Paul says,] "I urge you, first of all, to pray for all people. Ask God to help them; intercede on their behalf, and give thanks for them. . . . This is good and pleases God our Savior, who wants everyone to be saved and to understand the truth."

1 Timothy 2:1, 3-4

ADVERSITY

When it seems that nothing good could come of your circumstances . . .

[God says,] "Call on me when you are in trouble, and I will rescue you, and you will give me glory."

Psalm 50:15

We know that God causes everything to work together for the good of those who love God and are called according to his purpose for them.

Romans 8:28

Our present troubles are small and won't last very long. Yet they produce for us a glory that vastly outweighs them and will last forever!

2 Corinthians 4:17

When you need divine help . . .

God is our refuge and strength, always ready to help in times of trouble.
  Psalm 46:1

[God says,] "When you go through deep waters, I will be with you. When you go through rivers of difficulty, you will not drown. When you walk through the fire of oppression, you will not be burned up; the flames will not consume you. For I am the LORD, your God, the Holy One of Israel, your Savior."
  Isaiah 43:2-3

When it feels like you're on a slippery slope . . .

Give your burdens to the LORD, and he will take care of you. He will not permit the godly to slip and fall.
  Psalm 55:22

ADVICE

When you need advice for the mess you find yourself in . . .

Plans go wrong for lack of advice; many advisers bring success.
  Proverbs 15:22

Get all the advice and instruction you can, so you will be wise the rest of your life.
  Proverbs 19:20

ANGER

When you're furious with someone . . .

"Don't sin by letting anger control you." Don't let the sun go down while you are still angry, for anger gives a foothold to the devil.

Ephesians 4:26-27

When you're holding on to a grudge . . .

When you are praying, first forgive anyone you are holding a grudge against, so that your Father in heaven will forgive your sins, too.

Mark 11:25

If someone says, "I love God," but hates a Christian brother or sister, that person is a liar; for if we don't love people we can see, how can we love God, whom we cannot see?

1 John 4:20

When your anger is making the situation worse . . .

A gentle answer deflects anger, but harsh words make tempers flare.

Proverbs 15:1

ASSURANCE

When you find yourself in the gray areas of life . . .

The instructions of the LORD are perfect, reviving the soul.
The decrees of the LORD are trustworthy, making wise the
simple. The commandments of the LORD are right, bringing
joy to the heart. The commands of the LORD are clear, giving
insight for living.
Psalm 19:7-8

All [God] does is just and good, and all his commandments
are trustworthy. They are forever true, to be obeyed faithfully
and with integrity.
Psalm 111:7-8

When you doubt whether God will really save you . . .

[Jesus says,] "I tell you the truth, those who listen to my
message and believe in God who sent me have eternal life.
They will never be condemned for their sins, but they have
already passed from death into life."
John 5:24

**When you need to know that your faithfulness will be
rewarded . . .**

If we are faithful to the end, trusting God just as firmly
as when we first believed, we will share in all that belongs
to Christ.
Hebrews 3:14

ATTITUDE

When circumstances have worn you down and you need an attitude adjustment . . .

Be strong and courageous, and do the work. Don't be afraid or discouraged, for the LORD God . . . is with you. He will not fail you or forsake you. He will see to it that all the work . . . of the LORD is finished correctly.
1 Chronicles 28:20

My dear brothers and sisters, be strong and immovable. Always work enthusiastically for the Lord, for you know that nothing you do for the Lord is ever useless.
1 Corinthians 15:58

BLESSINGS

When you need a blessing in troubled times . . .

May the Lord of peace himself give you his peace at all times and in every situation. The Lord be with you.
2 Thessalonians 3:16

When you want to be a blessing in troubled times . . .

Don't repay evil for evil. Don't retaliate with insults when people insult you. Instead, pay them back with a blessing. That is what God has called you to do, and he will bless you for it.
1 Peter 3:9

BROKENHEARTED

When your hopes end in disappointment . . .

He lifted me out of the pit of despair, out of the mud and the mire. He set my feet on solid ground and steadied me as I walked along.

    Psalm 40:2

When doubts filled my mind, your comfort gave me renewed hope and cheer.

    Psalm 94:19

I pray that God, the source of hope, will fill you completely with joy and peace because you trust in him. Then you will overflow with confident hope through the power of the Holy Spirit.

    Romans 15:13

When you need your spirits lifted . . .

I will be glad and rejoice in your unfailing love, for you have seen my troubles, and you care about the anguish of my soul.

    Psalm 31:7

The LORD is close to the brokenhearted; he rescues those whose spirits are crushed.

    Psalm 34:18

As soon as I pray, you answer me; you encourage me by giving me strength.

    Psalm 138:3

BURNOUT

When you've been burning the candle at both ends . . .

It is useless for you to work so hard from early morning until late at night, anxiously working for food to eat; for God gives rest to his loved ones.
Psalm 127:2

When you feel overworked and overtired . . .

Those who live in the shelter of the Most High will find rest in the shadow of the Almighty.
Psalm 91:1

[God says,] "I have given rest to the weary."
Jeremiah 31:25

There is a special rest still waiting for the people of God. For all who have entered into God's rest have rested from their labors, just as God did after creating the world.
Hebrews 4:9-10

CHANGE

When changes keep moving you from one place to another . . .

O my Strength, to you I sing praises, for you, O God, are my refuge, the God who shows me unfailing love.
Psalm 59:17

I am certain that God, who began the good work within you, will continue his work until it is finally finished on the day when Christ Jesus returns.
Philippians 1:6

When you need something stable to cling to . . .

LORD, you remain the same forever! Your throne continues from generation to generation.
Lamentations 5:19

Jesus Christ is the same yesterday, today, and forever.
Hebrews 13:8

When one chapter closes and you're waiting for the next to begin . . .

God has made everything beautiful for its own time. He has planted eternity in the human heart, but even so, people cannot see the whole scope of God's work from beginning to end.
Ecclesiastes 3:11

When you need wisdom that will stand the test of time . . .

The grass withers and the flowers fade, but the word of our God stands forever.
Isaiah 40:8

CHAOS

When it feels like the world is crumbling to pieces . . .

The LORD is God, and he created the heavens and earth and put everything in place. He made the world to be lived in, not to be a place of empty chaos. "I am the LORD," he says, "and there is no other."
Isaiah 45:18

Through [Christ] God created everything in the heavenly realms and on earth. He made the things we can see and the things we can't see—such as thrones, kingdoms, rulers, and authorities in the unseen world. Everything was created through him and for him. He existed before anything else, and he holds all creation together.

Colossians 1:16-17

When there is just too much going on . . .

I am leaving you with a gift—peace of mind and heart. And the peace I give is a gift the world cannot give. So don't be troubled or afraid.

John 14:27

God is not a God of disorder but of peace, as in all the meetings of God's holy people.

1 Corinthians 14:33

May God give you more and more grace and peace as you grow in your knowledge of God and Jesus our Lord.

2 Peter 1:2

When you doubt God has a plan . . .

God has now revealed to us his mysterious plan regarding Christ, a plan to fulfill his own good pleasure. And this is the plan: At the right time he will bring everything together under the authority of Christ—everything in heaven and on earth.

Ephesians 1:9-10

CHARACTER

When you question whether God is who he says he is in the Bible . . .

How amazing are the deeds of the LORD! All who delight in him should ponder them. Everything he does reveals his glory and majesty. His righteousness never fails. He causes us to remember his wonderful works. How gracious and merciful is our LORD!

Psalm 111:2-4

When you doubt that having character matters . . .

Endurance develops strength of character, and character strengthens our confident hope of salvation. And this hope will not lead to disappointment. For we know how dearly God loves us, because he has given us the Holy Spirit to fill our hearts with his love.

Romans 5:4-5

We can be sure that we know him if we obey his commandments.

1 John 2:3

COMFORT

When you feel like a child who needs to be comforted . . .

The LORD is like a father to his children, tender and compassionate to those who fear him.

Psalm 103:13

Whenever you need help and consolation . . .

Let us come boldly to the throne of our gracious God. There
we will receive his mercy, and we will find grace to help us
when we need it most.

Hebrews 4:16

COURAGE

**When you need to be strong in the face of big
problems . . .**

I hold you by your right hand—I, the LORD your God. And
I say to you, "Don't be afraid. I am here to help you."

Isaiah 41:13

DEATH

When you've lost someone you love . . .

He will swallow up death forever! The Sovereign LORD will
wipe away all tears. He will remove forever all insults and
mockery against his land and people. The LORD has spoken!

Isaiah 25:8

When our dying bodies have been transformed into bodies
that will never die, this Scripture will be fulfilled: "Death
is swallowed up in victory. O death, where is your victory?
O death, where is your sting?"

1 Corinthians 15:54-55

When you doubt that there is life after death . . .

Those who die in the LORD will live; their bodies will rise again! Those who sleep in the earth will rise up and sing for joy! For your life-giving light will fall like dew on your people in the place of the dead!

Isaiah 26:19

God loved the world so much that he gave his one and only Son, so that everyone who believes in him will not perish but have eternal life.

John 3:16

When your life's end seems near . . .

[Jesus says,] "I tell you the truth, anyone who obeys my teaching will never die!"

John 8:51

Jesus told her, "I am the resurrection and the life. Anyone who believes in me will live, even after dying."

John 11:25

[John says,] "I heard a voice from heaven saying, 'Write this down: Blessed are those who die in the Lord from now on. Yes, says the Spirit, they are blessed indeed, for they will rest from their hard work; for their good deeds follow them!'"

Revelation 14:13

DECISIONS

When you need to know where to begin . . .

Seek his will in all you do, and he will show you which path to take.

Proverbs 3:6

When the right choice is a hard thing to do . . .

You will be accepted if you do what is right. But if you refuse to do what is right, then watch out! Sin is crouching at the door, eager to control you. But you must subdue it and be its master.
  Genesis 4:7

He renews my strength. He guides me along right paths, bringing honor to his name.
  Psalm 23:3

When you don't feel confident about your decisions . . .

If you need wisdom, ask our generous God, and he will give it to you. He will not rebuke you for asking. But when you ask him, be sure that your faith is in God alone. Do not waver, for a person with divided loyalty is as unsettled as a wave of the sea that is blown and tossed by the wind.
  James 1:5-6

When your bad choices have come back to haunt you . . .

"Come now, let's settle this," says the LORD. "Though your sins are like scarlet, I will make them as white as snow. Though they are red like crimson, I will make them as white as wool."
  Isaiah 1:18

I will give you a new heart, and I will put a new spirit in you. I will take out your stony, stubborn heart and give you a tender, responsive heart. And I will put my Spirit in you so that you will follow my decrees and be careful to obey my regulations.
  Ezekiel 36:26-27

Come back to the place of safety, all you . . . who still have hope! I promise this very day that I will repay two blessings for each of your troubles.

Zechariah 9:12

DEPRESSION

When all you see are dark days ahead . . .

Those who have been ransomed by the LORD will return. They will enter Jerusalem singing, crowned with everlasting joy. Sorrow and mourning will disappear, and they will be filled with joy and gladness.

Isaiah 35:10

God, who said, "Let there be light in the darkness," has made this light shine in our hearts so we could know the glory of God that is seen in the face of Jesus Christ.

2 Corinthians 4:6

When you feel invisible to God . . .

O LORD, you have examined my heart and know everything about me. You know when I sit down or stand up. You know my thoughts even when I'm far away. You see me when I travel and when I rest at home. You know everything I do. You know what I am going to say even before I say it, LORD. You go before me and follow me. You place your hand of blessing on my head.

Psalm 139:1-5

[Jesus says,] "This is the will of God, that I should not lose even one of all those he has given me, but that I should raise them up at the last day. For it is my Father's will that all who see his Son and believe in him should have eternal life. I will raise them up at the last day."

John 6:39-40

DISCERNMENT

When you're confused about which path to take . . .

Your word is a lamp to guide my feet and a light for my path.

Psalm 119:105

My child, don't lose sight of common sense and discernment. Hang on to them, for they will refresh your soul. They are like jewels on a necklace. They keep you safe on your way, and your feet will not stumble.

Proverbs 3:21-23

When you need to know what God wants you to do . . .

Give discernment to me, your servant; then I will understand your laws.

Psalm 119:125

O LORD, listen to my cry; give me the discerning mind you promised.

Psalm 119:169

DREAMS

When you desire things . . .

Enjoy what you have rather than desiring what you don't have. Just dreaming about nice things is meaningless—like chasing the wind.

Ecclesiastes 6:9

This world is fading away, along with everything that people crave. But anyone who does what pleases God will live forever.

1 John 2:17

When your dreams are crushed . . .

I cry out, "My splendor is gone! Everything I had hoped for from the LORD is lost!" . . . Yet I still dare to hope when I remember this: The faithful love of the LORD never ends! His mercies never cease. Great is his faithfulness; his mercies begin afresh each morning.

Lamentations 3:18, 21-23

ENDURANCE

When you feel as if you can't bear it any longer . . .

Patient endurance is what you need now, so that you will continue to do God's will. Then you will receive all that he has promised.

Hebrews 10:36

Dear brothers and sisters, when troubles come your way, consider it an opportunity for great joy. For you know that when your faith is tested, your endurance has a chance to grow. So let it grow, for when your endurance is fully developed, you will be perfect and complete, needing nothing.

James 1:2-4

God blesses those who patiently endure testing and temptation. Afterward they will receive the crown of life that God has promised to those who love him.

James 1:12

When you're having trouble keeping your eyes on Jesus . . .

Since we are surrounded by such a huge crowd of witnesses to the life of faith, let us strip off every weight that slows us down, especially the sin that so easily trips us up. And let us run with endurance the race God has set before us. We do this by keeping our eyes on Jesus, the champion who initiates and perfects our faith. Because of the joy awaiting him, he endured the cross, disregarding its shame. Now he is seated in the place of honor beside God's throne. Think of all the hostility he endured from sinful people; then you won't become weary and give up.

Hebrews 12:1-3

When you have resolved to press on . . .

Dear brothers and sisters, I have not achieved [perfection], but I focus on this one thing: Forgetting the past and looking forward to what lies ahead, I press on to reach the end of the race and receive the heavenly prize for which God, through Christ Jesus, is calling us.

Philippians 3:13-14

FAITH

When you have doubts that God's promises will be fulfilled . . .

God is not a man, so he does not lie. He is not human, so he does not change his mind. Has he ever spoken and failed to act? Has he ever promised and not carried it through?
Numbers 23:19

Faith is the confidence that what we hope for will actually happen; it gives us assurance about things we cannot see.
Hebrews 11:1

When you want to live by faith . . .

My old self has been crucified with Christ. It is no longer I who live, but Christ lives in me. So I live in this earthly body by trusting in the Son of God, who loved me and gave himself for me.
Galatians 2:20

Christ will make his home in your hearts as you trust in him. Your roots will grow down into God's love and keep you strong. And may you have the power to understand, as all God's people should, how wide, how long, how high, and how deep his love is. May you experience the love of Christ, though it is too great to understand fully. Then you will be made complete with all the fullness of life and power that comes from God.
Ephesians 3:17-19

When your faith is weak . . .

Just as you accepted Christ Jesus as your Lord, you must continue to follow him. Let your roots grow down into him, and let your lives be built on him. Then your faith will grow strong in the truth you were taught, and you will overflow with thankfulness.

Colossians 2:6-7

These trials will show that your faith is genuine. It is being tested as fire tests and purifies gold—though your faith is far more precious than mere gold. So when your faith remains strong through many trials, it will bring you much praise and glory and honor on the day when Jesus Christ is revealed to the whole world.

1 Peter 1:7

FEAR

When fear immobilizes you . . .

Do not be afraid or discouraged, for the LORD will personally go ahead of you. He will be with you; he will neither fail you nor abandon you.

Deuteronomy 31:8

Even when I walk through the darkest valley, I will not be afraid, for you are close beside me. Your rod and your staff protect and comfort me.

Psalm 23:4

When you need to take courage . . .

Don't be afraid, for I am with you. Don't be discouraged, for I am your God. I will strengthen you and help you. I will hold you up with my victorious right hand.
Isaiah 41:10

God has not given us a spirit of fear and timidity, but of power, love, and self-discipline.
2 Timothy 1:7

When you let God rule your life rather than fear . . .

We can say with confidence, "The LORD is my helper, so I will have no fear. What can mere people do to me?"
Hebrews 13:6

FINANCIAL HARDSHIP

When financial hardship or tragedy threatens to steal your dignity . . .

[The Lord made people] only a little lower than God and crowned them with glory and honor.
Psalm 8:5

The LORD says, "I will rescue those who love me. I will protect those who trust in my name. When they call on me, I will answer; I will be with them in trouble. I will rescue and honor them."
Psalm 91:14-15

When you're stressed about meeting your family's needs . . .

Don't worry about these things, saying, "What will we eat? What will we drink? What will we wear?" These things dominate the thoughts of unbelievers, but your heavenly Father already knows all your needs. Seek the Kingdom of God above all else, and live righteously, and he will give you everything you need.

Matthew 6:31-33

When you've lost everything you've worked so hard to acquire . . .

LORD, you alone are my inheritance, my cup of blessing. You guard all that is mine.

Psalm 16:5

Even though the fig trees have no blossoms, and there are no grapes on the vines; even though the olive crop fails, and the fields lie empty and barren; even though the flocks die in the fields, and the cattle barns are empty, yet I will rejoice in the LORD! I will be joyful in the God of my salvation!

Habakkuk 3:17-18

GOODNESS

When you need to know that God is good . . .

Let all that I am praise the LORD; may I never forget the good things he does for me. He forgives all my sins and heals all my diseases. He redeems me from death and crowns me with love and tender mercies. He fills my life with good things. My youth is renewed like the eagle's!

Psalm 103:2-5

Give thanks to the LORD, for he is good! His faithful love endures forever.

Psalm 106:1

How kind the LORD is! How good he is! So merciful, this God of ours! The LORD protects those of childlike faith; I was facing death, and he saved me. Let my soul be at rest again, for the LORD has been good to me.

Psalm 116:5-7

The LORD is good, a strong refuge when trouble comes. He is close to those who trust in him.

Nahum 1:7

GOOD NEWS

When you need to hear something uplifting . . .

God loved the world so much that he gave his one and only Son, so that everyone who believes in him will not perish but have eternal life. God sent his Son into the world not to judge the world, but to save the world through him.

John 3:16-17

We are here to bring you this Good News. The promise was made to our ancestors, and God has now fulfilled it for us, their descendants, by raising Jesus. . . . Brothers, listen! We are here to proclaim that through this man Jesus there is forgiveness for your sins.

Acts 13:32-33, 38

God promised this Good News long ago through his prophets in the holy Scriptures. The Good News is about his Son.

Romans 1:2-3

No eye has seen, no ear has heard, and no mind has imagined what God has prepared for those who love him.

1 Corinthians 2:9

Our present troubles are small and won't last very long. Yet they produce for us a glory that vastly outweighs them and will last forever!

2 Corinthians 4:17

[John says,] "I heard a loud shout from the throne, saying, 'Look, God's home is now among his people! He will live with them, and they will be his people. God himself will be with them. He will wipe every tear from their eyes, and there will be no more death or sorrow or crying or pain. All these things are gone forever.'"

Revelation 21:3-4

GRIEF

When your sorrows make you weary . . .

The LORD is close to the brokenhearted; he rescues those whose spirits are crushed.

Psalm 34:18

My health may fail, and my spirit may grow weak, but God remains the strength of my heart; he is mine forever.

Psalm 73:26

When you fear that more heartbreak is waiting . . .

The high and lofty one who lives in eternity, the Holy One, says this: "I live in the high and holy place with those whose spirits are contrite and humble. I restore the crushed spirit of the humble and revive the courage of those with repentant hearts."

Isaiah 57:15

[Jesus says,] "Don't let your hearts be troubled. Trust in God, and trust also in me."

John 14:1

When you don't have the words to comfort a grieving friend . . .

The Spirit of the LORD is upon me, for he has anointed me to bring Good News to the poor. He has sent me to proclaim that captives will be released, that the blind will see, that the oppressed will be set free.

Luke 4:18

All praise to God, the Father of our Lord Jesus Christ. God is our merciful Father and the source of all comfort. He comforts us in all our troubles so that we can comfort others. When they are troubled, we will be able to give them the same comfort God has given us.

2 Corinthians 1:3-4

When you don't know how to pray because life seems overwhelming . . .

The Holy Spirit helps us in our weakness. For example, we don't know what God wants us to pray for. But the Holy Spirit prays for us with groanings that cannot be expressed in words. And the Father who knows all hearts knows what the Spirit is saying, for the Spirit pleads for us believers in harmony with God's own will.

Romans 8:26-27

GUIDANCE

When you wish someone would show you the way . . .

With your unfailing love you lead the people you have redeemed. In your might, you guide them to your sacred home.

Exodus 15:13

The LORD says, "I will guide you along the best pathway for your life. I will advise you and watch over you."

Psalm 32:8

Jesus spoke to the people once more and said, "I am the light of the world. If you follow me, you won't have to walk in darkness, because you will have the light that leads to life."

John 8:12

When you're uncertain about the direction your life is taking . . .

[God] is our God forever and ever, and he will guide us until we die.

Psalm 48:14

The LORD will work out his plans for my life—for your faithful love, O LORD, endures forever.

Psalm 138:8

HELP

When you doubt that God wants to help you again and again . . .

From six disasters he will rescue you; even in the seventh, he will keep you from evil.

Job 5:19

Where is another God like you, who pardons the guilt of the remnant, overlooking the sins of his special people? You will not stay angry with your people forever, because you delight in showing unfailing love. Once again you will have compassion on us. You will trample our sins under your feet and throw them into the depths of the ocean!

Micah 7:18-19

When you can't lift yourself from the pit . . .

You light a lamp for me. The LORD, my God, lights up my darkness.

Psalm 18:28

The LORD opens the eyes of the blind. The LORD lifts up those who are weighed down. The LORD loves the godly.

Psalm 146:8

When trouble makes you feel helpless . . .

[Jesus says,] "I have told you all this so that you may have
peace in me. Here on earth you will have many trials and
sorrows. But take heart, because I have overcome the world."
John 16:33

HOPE

**When you need to believe that God has good plans for
your future . . .**

Show me the right path, O LORD; point out the road for me
to follow. Lead me by your truth and teach me, for you are
the God who saves me. All day long I put my hope in you.
Psalm 25:4-5

O Israel, hope in the LORD; for with the LORD there is
unfailing love. His redemption overflows.
Psalm 130:7

"I know the plans I have for you," says the LORD. "They are
plans for good and not for disaster, to give you a future and
a hope."
Jeremiah 29:11

When you feel hopeless . . .

Why am I discouraged? Why is my heart so sad? I will put
my hope in God! I will praise him again—my Savior and
my God!
Psalm 42:11

When you need to be reassured that eternity with Christ is real . . .

God wanted them to know that the riches and glory of Christ are for you Gentiles, too. And this is the secret: Christ lives in you. This gives you assurance of sharing his glory.
Colossians 1:27

Think clearly and exercise self-control. Look forward to the gracious salvation that will come to you when Jesus Christ is revealed to the world.
1 Peter 1:13

HUMILIATION

When your life feels like a march of shame . . .

Those who look to him for help will be radiant with joy; no shadow of shame will darken their faces.
Psalm 34:5

Thank God! He has made us his captives and continues to lead us along in Christ's triumphal procession.
2 Corinthians 2:14

Anyone who belongs to Christ has become a new person. The old life is gone; a new life has begun!
2 Corinthians 5:17

When the ways of this world bring you down . . .

Since you have been raised to new life with Christ, set your sights on the realities of heaven, where Christ sits in the place of honor at God's right hand. Think about the things of heaven, not the things of earth. For you died to this life, and your real life is hidden with Christ in God. And when Christ, who is your life, is revealed to the whole world, you will share in all his glory.

Colossians 3:1-4

INJUSTICE

When the whole world around you seems to be corrupt . . .

He will judge the world with justice and rule the nations with fairness. The LORD is a shelter for the oppressed, a refuge in times of trouble.

Psalm 9:8-9

The righteous LORD loves justice. The virtuous will see his face.

Psalm 11:7

When you strive to treat others with fairness . . .

There is joy for those who deal justly with others and always do what is right.

Psalm 106:3

When you need an advocate . . .

I will give repeated thanks to the LORD, praising him to everyone. For he stands beside the needy, ready to save them from those who condemn them.

Psalm 109:30-31

JESUS CHRIST

When you call on the name of Jesus . . .

Everyone who calls on the name of the LORD will be saved.
  Romans 10:13

When you want to be more like him . . .

All of us who have had that veil removed can see and reflect
the glory of the Lord. And the Lord—who is the Spirit—
makes us more and more like him as we are changed into his
glorious image.
  2 Corinthians 3:18

My old self has been crucified with Christ. It is no longer I
who live, but Christ lives in me. So I live in this earthly body
by trusting in the Son of God, who loved me and gave himself
for me.
  Galatians 2:20

When you wonder if Jesus really saves . . .

I am not ashamed of this Good News about Christ. It is the
power of God at work, saving everyone who believes.
  Romans 1:16

Jesus gave his life for our sins, just as God our Father planned,
in order to rescue us from this evil world in which we live.
  Galatians 1:4

He personally carried our sins in his body on the cross so
that we can be dead to sin and live for what is right. By his
wounds you are healed.
  1 Peter 2:24

JOY

When you feel as if you will never laugh again . . .

You will show me the way of life, granting me the joy of your presence and the pleasures of living with you forever.
Psalm 16:11

When you need your joy restored . . .

The commandments of the LORD are right, bringing joy to the heart. The commands of the LORD are clear, giving insight for living.
Psalm 19:8

Those who look to him for help will be radiant with joy; no shadow of shame will darken their faces. . . . Taste and see that the LORD is good. Oh, the joys of those who take refuge in him!
Psalm 34:5, 8

When you obey my commandments, you remain in my love, just as I obey my Father's commandments and remain in his love. I have told you these things so that you will be filled with my joy. Yes, your joy will overflow!
John 15:10-11

When you need a reason to be glad . . .

The LORD your God will delight in you if you obey his voice and keep the commands and decrees written in this Book of Instruction, and if you turn to the LORD your God with all your heart and soul.
Deuteronomy 30:10

The humble will see their God at work and be glad. Let all who seek God's help be encouraged.
Psalm 69:32

Songs of joy and victory are sung in the camp of the godly. The strong right arm of the LORD has done glorious things!
Psalm 118:15

I am overwhelmed with joy in the LORD my God! For he has dressed me with the clothing of salvation and draped me in a robe of righteousness. I am like a bridegroom in his wedding suit or a bride with her jewels.
Isaiah 61:10

LONELINESS

When you cannot feel God's presence . . .

I go east, but he is not there. I go west, but I cannot find him. I do not see him in the north, for he is hidden. I look to the south, but he is concealed. But he knows where I am going.
Job 23:8-10

I know the LORD is always with me. I will not be shaken, for he is right beside me.
Psalm 16:8

God has said, "I will never fail you. I will never abandon you."
Hebrews 13:5

Come close to God, and God will come close to you.
James 4:8

When you long for someone to talk to . . .

The LORD is a friend to those who fear him.
Psalm 25:14

[God says,] "When you pray, I will listen. If you look for me wholeheartedly, you will find me."
Jeremiah 29:12-13

Because of Christ and our faith in him, we can now come boldly and confidently into God's presence.
Ephesians 3:12

LOST

When it feels like you're fumbling your way through life . . .

The LORD directs the steps of the godly. He delights in every detail of their lives. Though they stumble . . . the LORD holds them by the hand.
Psalm 37:23-24

Your word is a lamp to guide my feet and a light for my path.
Psalm 119:105

When you wonder whether God remembers your hurts . . .

What is the price of five sparrows—two copper coins? Yet God does not forget a single one of them. And the very hairs on your head are all numbered. So don't be afraid; you are more valuable to God than a whole flock of sparrows.
Luke 12:6-7

LOVE

When you feel far removed from God's favor . . .

Surely your goodness and unfailing love will pursue me all the days of my life, and I will live in the house of the LORD forever.
Psalm 23:6

Can anything ever separate us from Christ's love? Does it mean he no longer loves us if we have trouble or calamity, or are persecuted, or hungry, or destitute, or in danger, or threatened with death? . . . No, despite all these things, overwhelming victory is ours through Christ, who loved us.

Romans 8:35, 37

[Paul says,] "I am convinced that nothing can ever separate us from God's love. Neither death nor life, neither angels nor demons, neither our fears for today nor our worries about tomorrow—not even the powers of hell can separate us from God's love. No power in the sky above or in the earth below—indeed, nothing in all creation will ever be able to separate us from the love of God that is revealed in Christ Jesus our Lord."

Romans 8:38-39

When you need to know how God really feels about you . . .

I will be glad and rejoice in your unfailing love, for you have seen my troubles, and you care about the anguish of my soul.

Psalm 31:7

The LORD is compassionate and merciful, slow to get angry and filled with unfailing love.

Psalm 103:8

How precious are your thoughts about me, O God.
They cannot be numbered! I can't even count them; they outnumber the grains of sand! And when I wake up, you are still with me!

Psalm 139:17-18

See how very much our Father loves us, for he calls us his children, and that is what we are!

1 John 3:1

When you wonder about the power of God's love . . .

[Jesus says,] "I am giving you a new commandment: Love each other. Just as I have loved you, you should love each other. Your love for one another will prove to the world that you are my disciples."

John 13:34-35

God showed how much he loved us by sending his one and only Son into the world so that we might have eternal life through him. This is real love—not that we loved God, but that he loved us and sent his Son as a sacrifice to take away our sins.

1 John 4:9-10

MONEY

When you want your investments to last forever . . .

Don't store up treasures here on earth, where moths eat them and rust destroys them, and where thieves break in and steal. Store your treasures in heaven, where moths and rust cannot destroy, and thieves do not break in and steal. Wherever your treasure is, there the desires of your heart will also be.

Matthew 6:19-21

Teach those who are rich in this world not to be proud and not to trust in their money, which is so unreliable. Their trust should be in God, who richly gives us all we need for our enjoyment. Tell them to use their money to do good. They should be rich in good works and generous to those in need, always being ready to share with others. By doing this they will be storing up their treasure as a good foundation for the future so that they may experience true life.

1 Timothy 6:17-19

When it hurts to give . . .

Better to have little, with fear for the LORD, than to have great treasure and inner turmoil.

Proverbs 15:16

Everyone who has given up houses or brothers or sisters or father or mother or children or property, for my sake, will receive a hundred times as much in return and will inherit eternal life.

Matthew 19:29

You must each decide in your heart how much to give. And don't give reluctantly or in response to pressure. "For God loves a person who gives cheerfully."

2 Corinthians 9:7

MOVING ON

When confusion about life keeps you from moving forward . . .

The LORD directs our steps, so why try to understand everything along the way?

Proverbs 20:24

Oh, how great are God's riches and wisdom and knowledge! How impossible it is for us to understand his decisions and his ways!

Romans 11:33

If you look carefully into the perfect law that sets you free, and if you do what it says and don't forget what you heard, then God will bless you for doing it.

James 1:25

When you need to move on and forget the past . . .

Oh, that we might know the LORD! Let us press on to know him. He will respond to us as surely as the arrival of dawn or the coming of rains in early spring.

Hosea 6:3

[Paul says,] "I focus on this one thing: Forgetting the past and looking forward to what lies ahead, I press on to reach the end of the race and receive the heavenly prize for which God, through Christ Jesus, is calling us."

Philippians 3:13-14

NEEDS

When you're worried that your needs won't be met . . .

[Paul says,] "This same God who takes care of me will supply all your needs from his glorious riches, which have been given to us in Christ Jesus."

Philippians 4:19

When you need to see the scope of God's care for you . . .

The LORD is my shepherd; I have all that I need. He lets me rest in green meadows; he leads me beside peaceful streams. He renews my strength. He guides me along right paths, bringing honor to his name.

Psalm 23:1-3

When you feel unequipped and inadequate to walk in God's ways . . .

By his divine power, God has given us everything we need for living a godly life. We have received all of this by coming to know him, the one who called us to himself by means of his marvelous glory and excellence. And because of his glory and excellence, he has given us great and precious promises. These are the promises that enable you to share his divine nature and escape the world's corruption caused by human desires.
2 Peter 1:3-4

OBEDIENCE

When doing the wrong thing could make your life easier . . .

Do not let sin control the way you live; do not give in to sinful desires.
Romans 6:12

Let's not get tired of doing what is good. At just the right time we will reap a harvest of blessing if we don't give up.
Galatians 6:9

Be careful then, dear brothers and sisters. Make sure that your own hearts are not evil and unbelieving, turning you away from the living God. You must warn each other every day, while it is still "today," so that none of you will be deceived by sin and hardened against God.
Hebrews 3:12-13

The eyes of the Lord watch over those who do right, and his ears are open to their prayers.
1 Peter 3:12

Anyone who wanders away from this teaching has no relationship with God. But anyone who remains in the teaching of Christ has a relationship with both the Father and the Son.

2 John 1:9

OBSTACLES

When you're feeling threatened by a challenging situation . . .

Do not be afraid of the terrors of the night, nor the arrow that flies in the day. Do not dread the disease that stalks in darkness, nor the disaster that strikes at midday. . . . The LORD says, "I will rescue those who love me. I will protect those who trust in my name."

Psalm 91:5-6, 14

I look up to the mountains—does my help come from there? My help comes from the LORD, who made heaven and earth!

Psalm 121:1-2

When a sinful habit trips you up . . .

Since we are surrounded by such a huge crowd of witnesses to the life of faith, let us strip off every weight that slows us down, especially the sin that so easily trips us up. And let us run with endurance the race God has set before us. We do this by keeping our eyes on Jesus, the champion who initiates and perfects our faith.

Hebrews 12:1-2

OPPOSITION

When you fear you are losing the battle . . .

Victory comes from you, O LORD. May you bless your
people.
Psalm 3:8

When it's time to face the enemy . . .

Be strong in the Lord and in his mighty power. Put on all of
God's armor so that you will be able to stand firm against all
strategies of the devil. For we are not fighting against flesh-
and-blood enemies, but against evil rulers and authorities of
the unseen world, against mighty powers in this dark world,
and against evil spirits in the heavenly places.
Ephesians 6:10-12

OVERCOMING

**When you are pushed to the limit, and you need God to
take it from here . . .**

Each one of you will put to flight a thousand of the enemy,
for the LORD your God fights for you, just as he has
promised.
Joshua 23:10

O LORD, I have so many enemies; so many are against me.
. . . But you, O LORD, are a shield around me; you are my
glory, the one who holds my head high. . . . Victory comes
from you, O LORD.
Psalm 3:1, 3, 8

The LORD always keeps his promises; he is gracious in all he does. The LORD helps the fallen and lifts those bent beneath their loads. The eyes of all look to you in hope. . . . The LORD is close to all who call on him, yes, to all who call on him in truth.

Psalm 145:13-15, 18

Don't be afraid, for I am with you. Don't be discouraged, for I am your God. I will strengthen you and help you. I will hold you up with my victorious right hand.

Isaiah 41:10

❧ PAIN

When you wonder if the pain will ever go away . . .

I will be glad and rejoice in your unfailing love, for you have seen my troubles, and you care about the anguish of my soul.

Psalm 31:7

Our present troubles are small and won't last very long. Yet they produce for us a glory that vastly outweighs them and will last forever!

2 Corinthians 4:17

In his kindness God called you to share in his eternal glory by means of Christ Jesus. So after you have suffered a little while, he will restore, support, and strengthen you, and he will place you on a firm foundation.

1 Peter 5:10

[God] will wipe every tear from their eyes, and there will be no more death or sorrow or crying or pain. All these things are gone forever.

Revelation 21:4

PANIC

When a crisis has paralyzed your ability to think straight . . .

God is our refuge and strength, always ready to help in times of trouble. So we will not fear when earthquakes come and the mountains crumble into the sea.
Psalm 46:1-2

[David says,] "Fear and trembling overwhelm me, and I can't stop shaking. . . . But I will call on God, and the LORD will rescue me."
Psalm 55:5, 16

[God says,] "When the earth quakes and its people live in turmoil, I am the one who keeps its foundations firm."
Psalm 75:3

Don't worry about anything; instead, pray about everything. Tell God what you need, and thank him for all he has done. Then you will experience God's peace, which exceeds anything we can understand. His peace will guard your hearts and minds as you live in Christ Jesus.
Philippians 4:6-7

PEACE

When you're looking for true peace . . .

The LORD gives his people strength. The LORD blesses them with peace.
Psalm 29:11

I listen carefully to what God the LORD is saying, for he speaks peace to his faithful people. But let them not return to their foolish ways.

Psalm 85:8

You will keep in perfect peace all who trust in you, all whose thoughts are fixed on you!

Isaiah 26:3

[Jesus says,] "I am leaving you with a gift—peace of mind and heart. And the peace I give is a gift the world cannot give. So don't be troubled or afraid."

John 14:27

When you wonder if the nations of this world will ever be at peace . . .

The LORD will mediate between nations and will settle international disputes. They will hammer their swords into plowshares and their spears into pruning hooks. Nation will no longer fight against nation, nor train for war anymore.

Isaiah 2:4

A child is born to us, a son is given to us. The government will rest on his shoulders. And he will be called: Wonderful Counselor, Mighty God, Everlasting Father, Prince of Peace. His government and its peace will never end.

Isaiah 9:6-7

Who will not fear you, Lord, and glorify your name? For you alone are holy. All nations will come and worship before you, for your righteous deeds have been revealed.

Revelation 15:4

PERSECUTION

When you are harassed or ill-treated because of your faith in Jesus . . .

God blesses you when people mock you and persecute you and lie about you and say all sorts of evil things against you because you are my followers. Be happy about it! Be very glad! For a great reward awaits you in heaven. And remember, the ancient prophets were persecuted in the same way.
   Matthew 5:11-12

The more we suffer for Christ, the more God will shower us with his comfort through Christ.
   2 Corinthians 1:5

When you're tempted to deny Christ . . .

Don't be afraid of what you are about to suffer. . . . But if you remain faithful even when facing death, I will give you the crown of life.
   Revelation 2:10

PERSEVERANCE

When you want your faith to be steady . . .

Those who love your instructions have great peace and do not stumble.
   Psalm 119:165

When you need a little hope to see you through a hard time . . .

Let us hold tightly without wavering to the hope we affirm, for God can be trusted to keep his promise.
Hebrews 10:23

When you persist in prayer . . .

Keep on asking, and you will receive what you ask for. Keep on seeking, and you will find. Keep on knocking, and the door will be opened to you. For everyone who asks, receives. Everyone who seeks, finds. And to everyone who knocks, the door will be opened.
Matthew 7:7-8

The earnest prayer of a righteous person has great power and produces wonderful results.
James 5:16

POVERTY

When you see someone in need . . .

Oh, the joys of those who are kind to the poor! The Lord rescues them when they are in trouble.
Psalm 41:1

Whoever gives to the poor will lack nothing, but those who close their eyes to poverty will be cursed.
Proverbs 28:27

When you find yourself without the basic necessities . . .

The needy will not be ignored forever; the hopes of the poor will not always be crushed.
Psalm 9:18

[God] lifts the poor from the dust and the needy from the garbage dump.

Psalm 113:7

When you feel spiritually destitute . . .

You know the generous grace of our Lord Jesus Christ. Though he was rich, yet for your sakes he became poor, so that by his poverty he could make you rich.

2 Corinthians 8:9

POWER OF GOD

When your troubles seem too big . . .

Mightier than the violent raging of the seas, mightier than the breakers on the shore—the LORD above is mightier than these!

Psalm 93:4

[Jesus] replied, "What is impossible for people is possible with God."

Luke 18:27

When you want to see the life-changing power of God in your life . . .

We now have this light shining in our hearts, but we ourselves are like fragile clay jars containing this great treasure. This makes it clear that our great power is from God, not from ourselves.

2 Corinthians 4:7

Each time [the Lord] said, "My grace is all you need. My power works best in weakness."

2 Corinthians 12:9

When you feel weakened by temptation . . .

God is working in you, giving you the desire and the power to do what pleases him.

Philippians 2:13

✺ PRAISE

When you need a reason to praise God in the tough times . . .

We can rejoice, too, when we run into problems and trials, for we know that they help us develop endurance. And endurance develops strength of character, and character strengthens our confident hope of salvation.

Romans 5:3-4

All glory to God, who is able to keep you from falling away and will bring you with great joy into his glorious presence without a single fault. All glory to him who alone is God, our Savior through Jesus Christ our Lord. All glory, majesty, power, and authority are his before all time, and in the present, and beyond all time! Amen.

Jude 1:24-25

When you testify to what God has done for you . . .

He has given me a new song to sing, a hymn of praise to our God. Many will see what he has done and be amazed. They will put their trust in the LORD.

Psalm 40:3

PRAYER

When you wonder if your prayers make a difference . . .

The earnest prayer of a righteous person has great power and
produces wonderful results.

James 5:16

When you need to know God hears you . . .

Morning, noon, and night I cry out in my distress, and the
Lord hears my voice.

Psalm 55:17

When you're waiting for God to answer . . .

I wait quietly before God, for my victory comes from him.
. . . Let all that I am wait quietly before God, for my hope is
in him. . . . O my people, trust in him at all times. Pour out
your heart to him, for God is our refuge.

Psalm 62:1, 5, 8

[God says,] "I will answer them before they even call to me.
While they are still talking about their needs, I will go ahead
and answer their prayers!"

Isaiah 65:24

If you sinful people know how to give good gifts to your
children, how much more will your heavenly Father give good
gifts to those who ask him.

Matthew 7:11

PRESENCE OF GOD

When you don't feel God's presence . . .

[God says,] "I will be your God throughout your lifetime—until your hair is white with age. I made you, and I will care for you. I will carry you along and save you."

Isaiah 46:4

When you wonder how God's presence touches your life . . .

You go before me and follow me. You place your hand of blessing on my head. Such knowledge is too wonderful for me, too great for me to understand! I can never escape from your Spirit! I can never get away from your presence! If I go up to heaven, you are there; if I go down to the grave, you are there. If I ride the wings of the morning, if I dwell by the farthest oceans, even there your hand will guide me, and your strength will support me.

Psalm 139:5-10

In all their suffering [God] also suffered, and he personally rescued them. In his love and mercy he redeemed them. He lifted them up and carried them through all the years.

Isaiah 63:9

PRESSURE

When your burdens become too heavy . . .

As pressure and stress bear down on me, I find joy in your commands.

Psalm 119:143

Jesus said, "Come to me, all of you who are weary and carry heavy burdens, and I will give you rest. Take my yoke upon you. Let me teach you, because I am humble and gentle at heart, and you will find rest for your souls. For my yoke is easy to bear, and the burden I give you is light."

Matthew 11:28-30

We are pressed on every side by troubles, but we are not crushed. We are perplexed, but not driven to despair. We are hunted down, but never abandoned by God. We get knocked down, but we are not destroyed. Through suffering, our bodies continue to share in the death of Jesus so that the life of Jesus may also be seen in our bodies.

2 Corinthians 4:8-10

PRIDE

When you feel God doesn't need to forgive you for anything . . .

If we claim we have no sin, we are only fooling ourselves and not living in the truth. But if we confess our sins to him, he is faithful and just to forgive us our sins and to cleanse us from all wickedness.

1 John 1:8-9

When you want to be recognized for the good things you do . . .

[Jesus] said to them, "You like to appear righteous in public, but God knows your hearts. What this world honors is detestable in the sight of God."

Luke 16:15

The Scriptures say, "If you want to boast, boast only about the LORD." When people commend themselves, it doesn't count for much. The important thing is for the Lord to commend them.

2 Corinthians 10:17-18

When you wonder how to avoid pride in your life . . .

All who fear the LORD will hate evil. Therefore, I hate pride and arrogance, corruption and perverse speech.

Proverbs 8:13

[Jesus] said, "Whoever wants to be first must take last place and be the servant of everyone else."

Mark 9:35

PRISONERS

When you feel cut off from God . . .

The LORD hears the cries of the needy; he does not despise his imprisoned people.

Psalm 69:33

When you've been captured by a sinful habit . . .

He gives justice to the oppressed and food to the hungry. The Lord frees the prisoners.

Psalm 146:7

He gave his life to free us from every kind of sin, to cleanse us, and to make us his very own people, totally committed to doing good deeds.

Titus 2:14

PROMISES OF GOD

When you're tired of empty promises . . .

"The mountains may move and the hills disappear, but even then my faithful love for you will remain. My covenant of blessing will never be broken," says the LORD, who has mercy on you.

Isaiah 54:10

When you question whether God's promises are meant for you . . .

God's way is perfect. All the LORD's promises prove true. He is a shield for all who look to him for protection.

Psalm 18:30

Now that you belong to Christ, you are the true children of Abraham. You are his heirs, and God's promise to Abraham belongs to you.

Galatians 3:29

When you wonder whether God keeps his promises . . .

We are here to bring you this Good News. The promise was made to our ancestors, and God has now fulfilled it for us, their descendants, by raising Jesus. This is what the second psalm says about Jesus: "You are my Son. Today I have become your Father." For God had promised to raise him from the dead, not leaving him to rot in the grave. He said, "I will give you the sacred blessings I promised to David."

Acts 13:32-34

Jesus Christ, the Son of God, does not waver between "Yes" and "No." He is the one whom Silas, Timothy, and I preached to you, and as God's ultimate "Yes," he always does what he says. For all of God's promises have been fulfilled in Christ with a resounding "Yes!" And through Christ, our "Amen" (which means "Yes") ascends to God for his glory.

2 Corinthians 1:19-20

PROTECTION

When the enemy aims his arrows at you . . .

The LORD is my strength and shield. I trust him with all my heart. He helps me, and my heart is filled with joy. I burst out in songs of thanksgiving.

Psalm 28:7

When you need to take cover from life's storms . . .

Those who live in the shelter of the Most High will find rest in the shadow of the Almighty. This I declare about the LORD: He alone is my refuge, my place of safety; he is my God, and I trust him. For he will rescue you. . . . He will cover you. . . . He will shelter you. . . . His faithful promises are your armor and protection. Do not be afraid of the terrors of the night, nor the arrow that flies in the day. . . . Though a thousand fall at your side, though ten thousand are dying around you, these evils will not touch you. . . . For he will order his angels to protect you wherever you go.

Psalm 91:1-5, 7, 11

The name of the LORD is a strong fortress; the godly run to him and are safe.

Proverbs 18:10

When you need someone to defend you . . .

The LORD your God fights for you, just as he has promised.
So be very careful to love the LORD your God.
  Joshua 23:10-11

He will protect his faithful ones, but the wicked will disappear
in darkness.
  1 Samuel 2:9

My help comes from the LORD, who made heaven and earth!
He will not let you stumble; the one who watches over you
will not slumber. Indeed, he who watches over Israel never
slumbers or sleeps. The LORD himself watches over you! The
LORD stands beside you as your protective shade. . . . The
LORD keeps watch over you as you come and go, both now
and forever.
  Psalm 121:2-5, 8

REBELLION

When someone you love rebels against God . . .

Most important of all, continue to show deep love for each
other, for love covers a multitude of sins.
  1 Peter 4:8

When you're tired of resisting God . . .

The Lord our God is merciful and forgiving, even though
we have rebelled against him.
  Daniel 9:9

When you think your past makes you unworthy of serving Christ . . .

God was in Christ, reconciling the world to himself, no longer counting people's sins against them. And he gave us this wonderful message of reconciliation.

2 Corinthians 5:19

[God] canceled the record of the charges against us and took it away by nailing it to the cross.

Colossians 2:14

RENEWAL

When your old way of living has left you feeling spiritually dull and dead inside . . .

Our great desire is that you will keep on loving others as long as life lasts, in order to make certain that what you hope for will come true. Then you will not become spiritually dull and indifferent. Instead, you will follow the example of those who are going to inherit God's promises because of their faith and endurance.

Hebrews 6:11-12

REST

When anxious thoughts disturb your sleep . . .

I lay down and slept, yet I woke up in safety, for the LORD was watching over me.

Psalm 3:5

When you need relief from your struggles . . .

Jesus said, "Come to me, all of you who are weary and carry heavy burdens, and I will give you rest."
   Matthew 11:28

When you need a supernatural energy boost . . .

He gives power to the weak and strength to the powerless. Even youths will become weak and tired, and young men will fall in exhaustion. But those who trust in the LORD will find new strength. They will soar high on wings like eagles. They will run and not grow weary. They will walk and not faint.
   Isaiah 40:29-31

SAFETY

When you need someone to watch over you . . .

The LORD himself watches over you! The LORD stands beside you as your protective shade. The sun will not harm you by day, nor the moon at night. The LORD keeps you from all harm and watches over your life. The LORD keeps watch over you as you come and go, both now and forever.
   Psalm 121:5-8

When it feels like your world is shaking . . .

I know the LORD is always with me. I will not be shaken, for he is right beside me. No wonder my heart is glad, and I rejoice. My body rests in safety.
   Psalm 16:8-9

SECURITY

When it seems the enemy is closing in on you . . .

Those who trust in the Lord are as secure as Mount Zion; they will not be defeated but will endure forever. Just as the mountains surround Jerusalem, so the Lord surrounds his people, both now and forever.

Psalm 125:1-2

When you search for security in anything other than God . . .

Unless the Lord builds a house, the work of the builders is wasted. Unless the Lord protects a city, guarding it with sentries will do no good.

Psalm 127:1

SICKNESS

When your health is failing . . .

My health may fail, and my spirit may grow weak, but God remains the strength of my heart; he is mine forever.

Psalm 73:26

O Lord, if you heal me, I will be truly healed; if you save me, I will be truly saved. My praises are for you alone!

Jeremiah 17:14

For you who fear my name, the Sun of Righteousness will rise with healing in his wings. And you will go free, leaping with joy like calves let out to pasture.

Malachi 4:2

[John says,] "I heard a loud shout from the throne, saying, 'Look, God's home is now among his people! He will live with them, and they will be his people. God himself will be with them. He will wipe every tear from their eyes, and there will be no more death or sorrow or crying or pain. All these things are gone forever.'"

Revelation 21:3-4

When you want to be spiritually fit . . .

Do not waste time arguing over godless ideas and old wives' tales. Instead, train yourself to be godly. "Physical training is good, but training for godliness is much better, promising benefits in this life and in the life to come."

1 Timothy 4:7-8

SIN

When you haven't lived according to God's teachings . . .

Get rid of all the filth and evil in your lives, and humbly accept the word God has planted in your hearts, for it has the power to save your souls.

James 1:21

When you fall short . . .

[David said,] "Finally, I confessed all my sins to you and stopped trying to hide my guilt. I said to myself, 'I will confess my rebellion to the LORD.' And you forgave me! All my guilt is gone."

Psalm 32:5

People who conceal their sins will not prosper, but if they confess and turn from them, they will receive mercy.
Proverbs 28:13

Everyone has sinned; we all fall short of God's glorious standard. Yet God, with undeserved kindness, declares that we are righteous. He did this through Christ Jesus when he freed us from the penalty for our sins.
Romans 3:23-24

If we confess our sins to him, he is faithful and just to forgive us our sins and to cleanse us.
1 John 1:9

When it seems your guilt will follow you forever . . .

[The Lord says,] "I—yes, I alone—will blot out your sins for my own sake and will never think of them again."
Isaiah 43:25

When you can't imagine that God could forgive you . . .

O Lord, you are so good, so ready to forgive, so full of unfailing love for all who ask for your help.
Psalm 86:5

"Come now, let's settle this," says the LORD. "Though your sins are like scarlet, I will make them as white as snow. Though they are red like crimson, I will make them as white as wool."
Isaiah 1:18

There is forgiveness of sins for all who repent.
Luke 24:47

SORROW

When you wonder whether the journey through this life will be worth it . . .

Those who have been ransomed by the LORD will return. They will enter Jerusalem singing, crowned with everlasting joy. Sorrow and mourning will disappear, and they will be filled with joy and gladness.
Isaiah 35:10

SPIRITUAL DRYNESS

When your faith has withered . . .

The LORD will guide you continually, giving you water when you are dry and restoring your strength. You will be like a well-watered garden, like an ever-flowing spring.
Isaiah 58:11

When it feels as if God has hidden himself from you . . .

You will search again for the LORD your God. And if you search for him with all your heart and soul, you will find him.
Deuteronomy 4:29

The LORD will stay with you as long as you stay with him! Whenever you seek him, you will find him. But if you abandon him, he will abandon you.
2 Chronicles 15:2

When your heart feels cold and resistant toward God . . .

I will give them singleness of heart and put a new spirit within them. I will take away their stony, stubborn heart and give them a tender, responsive heart, so they will obey my decrees and regulations.
Ezekiel 11:19-20

Plant the good seeds of righteousness, and you will harvest a crop of love. Plow up the hard ground of your hearts, for now is the time to seek the LORD, that he may come and shower righteousness upon you.
Hosea 10:12

SPIRITUAL WARFARE

When you wonder if evil is real . . .

We are not fighting against flesh-and-blood enemies, but against evil rulers and authorities of the unseen world, against mighty powers in this dark world, and against evil spirits in the heavenly places.
Ephesians 6:12

When you need a weapon to protect yourself from spiritual attack . . .

The word of God is alive and powerful. It is sharper than the sharpest two-edged sword, cutting between soul and spirit, between joint and marrow. It exposes our innermost thoughts and desires. Nothing in all creation is hidden from God. Everything is naked and exposed before his eyes, and he is the one to whom we are accountable.
Hebrews 4:12-13

Because of his glory and excellence, he has given us great and precious promises. These are the promises that enable you to share his divine nature and escape the world's corruption caused by human desires.
    2 Peter 1:4

When you need supernatural protection . . .

My victory and honor come from God alone. He is my refuge, a rock where no enemy can reach me.
    Psalm 62:7

If you make the LORD your refuge, if you make the Most High your shelter, no evil will conquer you; no plague will come near your home. For he will order his angels to protect you wherever you go. They will hold you up with their hands so you won't even hurt your foot on a stone. You will trample upon lions and cobras; you will crush fierce lions and serpents under your feet!
    Psalm 91:9-13

When you want to be on the winning side . . .

You who love the LORD, hate evil! He protects the lives of his godly people and rescues them from the power of the wicked.
    Psalm 97:10

Be strong in the Lord and in his mighty power. Put on all of God's armor so that you will be able to stand firm against all strategies of the devil.
    Ephesians 6:10-11

STRANDED

When it feels as if God has abandoned you . . .

The LORD will not abandon his people, because that would dishonor his great name. For it has pleased the LORD to make you his very own people.

1 Samuel 12:22

I will not abandon you as orphans—I will come to you.

John 14:18

When you feel stuck in a place you don't want to be . . .

I cry out to God Most High, to God who will fulfill his purpose for me. He will send help from heaven to rescue me, disgracing those who hound me.

Psalm 57:2-3

This is what the LORD says: "Stop at the crossroads and look around. Ask for the old, godly way, and walk in it. Travel its path, and you will find rest for your souls."

Jeremiah 6:16

This is what the Sovereign LORD says: I myself will search and find my sheep. I will be like a shepherd looking for his scattered flock. I will find my sheep and rescue them from all the places where they were scattered on that dark and cloudy day.

Ezekiel 34:11-12

SUFFERING

When your troubles are too heavy to bear . . .

You keep track of all my sorrows. You have collected all my tears in your bottle. You have recorded each one in your book.
Psalm 56:8

You have allowed me to suffer much hardship, but you will restore me to life again and lift me up from the depths of the earth. You will restore me to even greater honor and comfort me once again.
Psalm 71:20-21

The LORD helps the fallen and lifts those bent beneath their loads.
Psalm 145:14

When you wonder what good can come from your suffering . . .

I am glad to boast about my weaknesses, so that the power of Christ can work through me. That's why I take pleasure in my weaknesses, and in the insults, hardships, persecutions, and troubles that I suffer for Christ. For when I am weak, then I am strong.
2 Corinthians 12:9-10

Don't be surprised at the fiery trials you are going through, as if something strange were happening to you. Instead, be very glad—for these trials make you partners with Christ in his suffering, so that you will have the wonderful joy of seeing his glory when it is revealed to all the world.
1 Peter 4:12-13

When you need comfort . . .

Even when I walk through the darkest valley, I will not be afraid, for you are close beside me. Your rod and your staff protect and comfort me.

Psalm 23:4

Sing for joy, O heavens! Rejoice, O earth! Burst into song, O mountains! For the LORD has comforted his people and will have compassion on them in their suffering.

Isaiah 49:13

When it is your turn to comfort someone who is suffering . . .

All praise to God, the Father of our Lord Jesus Christ. God is our merciful Father and the source of all comfort. He comforts us in all our troubles so that we can comfort others. When they are troubled, we will be able to give them the same comfort God has given us.

2 Corinthians 1:3-4

℅ TEMPTATION

When you wonder if you can resist . . .

If you think you are standing strong, be careful not to fall. The temptations in your life are no different from what others experience. And God is faithful. He will not allow the temptation to be more than you can stand. When you are tempted, he will show you a way out so that you can endure.

1 Corinthians 10:12-13

The Lord is faithful; he will strengthen you and guard you from the evil one.

2 Thessalonians 3:3

When you feel as if no one understands how hard you are trying . . .

Since [Jesus] himself has gone through suffering and testing, he is able to help us when we are being tested.
Hebrews 2:18

This High Priest of ours understands our weaknesses, for he faced all of the same testings we do, yet he did not sin.
Hebrews 4:15

TERRORISM

When evil people intimidate you and plot violence . . .

He ransoms me and keeps me safe from the battle waged against me, though many still oppose me.
Psalm 55:18

Yes, the LORD is for me; he will help me. I will look in triumph at those who hate me.
Psalm 118:7

When you live in fear of those who want to harm you . . .

The LORD is my light and my salvation—so why should I be afraid? The LORD is my fortress, protecting me from danger, so why should I tremble? . . . Though a mighty army surrounds me, my heart will not be afraid. Even if I am attacked, I will remain confident.
Psalm 27:1, 3

When I am afraid, I will put my trust in you. I praise God for what he has promised. I trust in God, so why should I be afraid? What can mere mortals do to me?
Psalm 56:3-4

Don't be afraid of those who want to kill your body; they cannot touch your soul. Fear only God, who can destroy both soul and body in hell.
Matthew 10:28

When you remember those who have been harmed . . .

God blesses those who mourn, for they will be comforted.
Matthew 5:4

TESTING

When you fear your trials will crush your faith . . .

God blesses those who patiently endure testing and temptation. Afterward they will receive the crown of life that God has promised to those who love him. And remember, when you are being tempted, do not say, "God is tempting me." God is never tempted to do wrong, and he never tempts anyone else.
James 1:12-13

Trials will show that your faith is genuine. It is being tested as fire tests and purifies gold—though your faith is far more precious than mere gold. So when your faith remains strong through many trials, it will bring you much praise and glory and honor on the day when Jesus Christ is revealed to the whole world.
1 Peter 1:7

When there are impure motives in your heart . . .

Fire tests the purity of silver and gold, but the LORD tests the heart.
Proverbs 17:3

When you want to be strong enough for anything . . .

You know that when your faith is tested, your endurance has
a chance to grow.
  James 1:3

TIMING OF GOD

When it seems as if God is late . . .

This vision is for a future time. It describes the end, and it
will be fulfilled. If it seems slow in coming, wait patiently,
for it will surely take place. It will not be delayed.
  Habakkuk 2:3

The Lord isn't really being slow about his promise, as some
people think. No, he is being patient for your sake. He
does not want anyone to be destroyed, but wants everyone
to repent.
  2 Peter 3:9

**When you're trying to make things happen in your own
time . . .**

We can make our plans, but the LORD determines our steps.
  Proverbs 16:9

The LORD of Heaven's Armies has spoken—who can change
his plans? When his hand is raised, who can stop him?
  Isaiah 14:27

When you see God's perfect timing . . .

O LORD, I will honor and praise your name, for you are my
God. You do such wonderful things! You planned them long
ago, and now you have accomplished them.
  Isaiah 25:1

When you long for Christ to return . . .

Dear brothers and sisters, be patient as you wait for the Lord's return. Consider the farmers who patiently wait for the rains in the fall and in the spring. They eagerly look for the valuable harvest to ripen. You, too, must be patient. Take courage, for the coming of the Lord is near.

James 5:7-8

TROUBLE

When you long for good days to return . . .

You have allowed me to suffer much hardship, but you will restore me to life again and lift me up from the depths of the earth. You will restore me to even greater honor and comfort me once again.

Psalm 71:20-21

When you don't know what else to do . . .

I will call to you whenever I'm in trouble, and you will answer me.

Psalm 86:7

As for me, I look to the LORD for help. I wait confidently for God to save me, and my God will certainly hear me. Do not gloat over me, my enemies! For though I fall, I will rise again. Though I sit in darkness, the LORD will be my light.

Micah 7:7-8

TRUSTING

When you need to know that God will be faithful . . .

Understand, therefore, that the LORD your God is indeed God. He is the faithful God who keeps his covenant for a thousand generations and lavishes his unfailing love on those who love him and obey his commands.

Deuteronomy 7:9

Many sorrows come to the wicked, but unfailing love surrounds those who trust the LORD.

Psalm 32:10

When you are afraid that God's patience will run out . . .

Your unfailing love, O LORD, is as vast as the heavens; your faithfulness reaches beyond the clouds. Your righteousness is like the mighty mountains, your justice like the ocean depths. You care for people and animals alike, O LORD.

Psalm 36:5-6

When your confidence in the Lord is shaken . . .

Blessed are those who trust in the LORD and have made the LORD their hope and confidence.

Jeremiah 17:7

If we are faithful to the end, trusting God just as firmly as when we first believed, we will share in all that belongs to Christ.

Hebrews 3:14

When you're ready to step out in faith . . .

Commit everything you do to the LORD. Trust him, and he will help you.

Psalm 37:5

VIOLENCE

When you're shocked by how violent people can be . . .

The Lord examines both the righteous and the wicked. He hates those who love violence.

Psalm 11:5

The Lord replies, "I have seen violence done to the helpless, and I have heard the groans of the poor. Now I will rise up to rescue them, as they have longed for me to do."

Psalm 12:5

When you wonder if the power of Christ is enough to overcome evil . . .

The Lord is faithful; he will strengthen you and guard you from the evil one.

2 Thessalonians 3:3

The Lord will deliver me from every evil attack and will bring me safely into his heavenly Kingdom.

2 Timothy 4:18

You belong to God, my dear children. You have already won a victory over those people, because the Spirit who lives in you is greater than the spirit who lives in the world.

1 John 4:4

Every child of God defeats this evil world, and we achieve this victory through our faith. And who can win this battle against the world? Only those who believe that Jesus is the Son of God.

1 John 5:4-5

⚞ WEAKNESS

When your circumstances make you weak . . .

We now have this light shining in our hearts, but we ourselves are like fragile clay jars containing this great treasure. This makes it clear that our great power is from God, not from ourselves.

2 Corinthians 4:7

When you wonder why God doesn't always take away your troubles . . .

My grace is all you need. My power works best in weakness.

2 Corinthians 12:9

⚞ WILL OF GOD

When you're having trouble discerning God's will for your life . . .

Don't copy the behavior and customs of this world, but let God transform you into a new person by changing the way you think. Then you will learn to know God's will for you, which is good and pleasing and perfect.

Romans 12:2

When following God's will seems impossibly hard . . .

"I know the plans I have for you," says the LORD. "They are plans for good and not for disaster, to give you a future and a hope."

Jeremiah 29:11

WISDOM

When you need good judgment in tough situations . . .

Fear of the LORD is the foundation of true wisdom. All who obey his commandments will grow in wisdom.

Psalm 111:10

Come and listen to my counsel. I'll share my heart with you and make you wise.

Proverbs 1:23

Knowledge of the Holy One results in good judgment.

Proverbs 9:10

If you need wisdom, ask our generous God, and he will give it to you. He will not rebuke you for asking.

James 1:5

WORD OF GOD

When you crave spiritual food . . .

The laws of the LORD are true; each one is fair. They are more desirable than gold, even the finest gold. They are sweeter than honey, even honey dripping from the comb. They are a warning to your servant, a great reward for those who obey them.

Psalm 19:9-11

When I discovered your words, I devoured them. They are my joy and my heart's delight, for I bear your name, O LORD God of Heaven's Armies.

Jeremiah 15:16

When you want to build your trust on things eternal . . .

Your eternal word, O LORD, stands firm in heaven.
   Psalm 119:89

Heaven and earth will disappear, but my words will never disappear.
   Matthew 24:35

When you need life-changing counsel . . .

All Scripture is inspired by God and is useful to teach us what is true and to make us realize what is wrong in our lives. It corrects us when we are wrong and teaches us to do what is right. God uses it to prepare and equip his people to do every good work.
   2 Timothy 3:16-17

The word of God is alive and powerful. It is sharper than the sharpest two-edged sword, cutting between soul and spirit, between joint and marrow. It exposes our innermost thoughts and desires.
   Hebrews 4:12

When you want to know the benefits of reading God's Word . . .

[God says,] "The rain and snow come down from the heavens and stay on the ground to water the earth. They cause the grain to grow, producing seed for the farmer and bread for the hungry. It is the same with my word. I send it out, and it always produces fruit. It will accomplish all I want it to, and it will prosper everywhere I send it."
   Isaiah 55:10-11

Jesus replied, "But even more blessed are all who hear the word of God and put it into practice."
   Luke 11:28

WORK

When you fear your efforts won't be enough . . .

Be strong and courageous, for your work will be rewarded.
2 Chronicles 15:7

When you long to be useful . . .

My dear brothers and sisters, be strong and immovable. Always work enthusiastically for the Lord, for you know that nothing you do for the Lord is ever useless.
1 Corinthians 15:58

When you wonder whether God has quit working in you . . .

[Paul says,] "I am certain that God, who began the good work within you, will continue his work until it is finally finished on the day when Christ Jesus returns."
Philippians 1:6

WORRY

When you can't push your worries from your mind . . .

Don't worry about anything; instead, pray about everything. Tell God what you need, and thank him for all he has done. Then you will experience God's peace, which exceeds anything we can understand. His peace will guard your hearts and minds as you live in Christ Jesus.
Philippians 4:6-7 ·

Give all your worries and cares to God, for he cares about you.
1 Peter 5:7

WORSHIP

When this world seems like a godless place . . .

Everything on earth will worship you; they will sing your praises, shouting your name in glorious songs.
   Psalm 66:4

When you don't feel like worshiping . . .

It is good to give thanks to the LORD, to sing praises to the Most High.
   Psalm 92:1

Come close to God, and God will come close to you.
   James 4:8

When you want to recognize God's presence . . .

Come, let us worship and bow down. Let us kneel before the LORD our maker, for he is our God. We are the people he watches over, the flock under his care.
   Psalm 95:6-7

Who will not fear you, Lord, and glorify your name? For you alone are holy. All nations will come and worship before you, for your righteous deeds have been revealed.
   Revelation 15:4

When you can't contain your joy for the Lord . . .

You thrill me, LORD, with all you have done for me! I sing for joy because of what you have done.
   Psalm 92:4

⚜ FAVORITE VERSES ⚜

⚜ When you feel as if God has abandoned you . . .

Those who know your name trust in you, for you, O LORD,
do not abandon those who search for you.
Psalm 9:10

⚜ When you've been harmed . . .

We are hunted down, but never abandoned by God. We get
knocked down, but we are not destroyed.
2 Corinthians 4:9

⚜ When healing seems impossible . . .

He heals the brokenhearted and bandages their wounds.
Psalm 147:3

⚜ When you've been falsely accused . . .

Be careful to live properly among your unbelieving neighbors.
Then even if they accuse you of doing wrong, they will see
your honorable behavior, and they will give honor to God
when he judges the world.
1 Peter 2:12

When you struggle with addiction . . .

Do not let sin control the way you live; do not give in to sinful desires. Do not let any part of your body become an instrument of evil to serve sin. Instead, give yourselves completely to God, for you were dead, but now you have new life. So use your whole body as an instrument to do what is right for the glory of God. Sin is no longer your master, for you no longer live under the requirements of the law. Instead, you live under the freedom of God's grace.

Romans 6:12-14

When it seems that nothing good could come of your circumstances . . .

Call on me when you are in trouble, and I will rescue you, and you will give me glory.

Psalm 50:15

When you need help . . .

God is our refuge and strength, always ready to help in times of trouble.

Psalm 46:1

Come back to the place of safety . . . all you . . . who still have hope! I promise this very day that I will repay two blessings for each of your troubles!

Zechariah 9:12

When circumstances have worn you down and you need an attitude adjustment . . .

Be strong and courageous, and do the work. Don't be afraid or discouraged, for the LORD God . . . is with you. He will not fail you or forsake you. He will see to it that all the work . . . of the LORD is finished correctly.

1 Chronicles 28:20

When your hopes end in disappointment . . .

The LORD is close to the brokenhearted; he rescues those
whose spirits are crushed.
Psalm 34:18

He lifted me out of the pit of despair, out of the mud and
the mire. He set my feet on solid ground and steadied me
as I walked along.
Psalm 40:2

I pray that God, the source of hope, will fill you completely
with joy and peace because you trust in him. Then you will
overflow with confident hope through the power of the
Holy Spirit.
Romans 15:13

When you feel overworked and overtired . . .

Those who live in the shelter of the Most High will find rest
in the shadow of the Almighty.
Psalm 91:1

When you need something stable to cling to . . .

LORD, you remain the same forever! Your throne continues
from generation to generation.
Lamentations 5:19

When there is just too much going on . . .

I am leaving you with a gift—peace of mind and heart. And
the peace I give is a gift the world cannot give. So don't be
troubled or afraid.
John 14:27

When you need to be strong in the face of big problems . . .

I hold you by your right hand—I, the LORD your God. And I say to you, "Don't be afraid. I am here to help you."
Isaiah 41:13

When you've lost someone you love . . .

He will swallow up death forever! The Sovereign LORD will wipe away all tears.
Isaiah 25:8

When your life's end seems near . . .

Jesus told her, "I am the resurrection and the life. Anyone who believes in me will live, even after dying."
John 11:25

When you don't feel confident about your decisions . . .

If you need wisdom, ask our generous God, and he will give it to you. He will not rebuke you for asking. But when you ask him, be sure that your faith is in God alone. Do not waver, for a person with divided loyalty is as unsettled as a wave of the sea that is blown and tossed by the wind.
James 1:5-6

When you feel invisible to God . . .

O LORD, you have examined my heart and know everything about me. You know when I sit down or stand up. You know my thoughts even when I'm far away. You see me when I travel and when I rest at home. You know everything I do. You know what I am going to say even before I say it, LORD. You go before me and follow me. You place your hand of blessing on my head.
Psalm 139:1-5

When you need to know what God wants you to do . . .

O LORD, listen to my cry; give me the discerning mind you promised.

Psalm 119:169

When your dreams are crushed . . .

I cry out, "My splendor is gone! Everything I had hoped for from the LORD is lost!" . . . Yet I still dare to hope when I remember this: The faithful love of the LORD never ends! His mercies never cease. Great is his faithfulness; his mercies begin afresh each morning.

Lamentations 3:18, 21-23

When you feel as if you can't bear it any longer . . .

Dear brothers and sisters, when troubles come your way, consider it an opportunity for great joy. For you know that when your faith is tested, your endurance has a chance to grow. So let it grow, for when your endurance is fully developed, you will be perfect and complete, needing nothing.

James 1:2-4

When you want to live by faith . . .

Christ will make his home in your hearts as you trust in him. Your roots will grow down into God's love and keep you strong. And may you have the power to understand, as all God's people should, how wide, how long, how high, and how deep his love is. May you experience the love of Christ, though it is too great to understand fully. Then you will be made complete with all the fullness of life and power that comes from God.

Ephesians 3:17-19

When fear immobilizes you . . .

Do not be afraid or discouraged, for the LORD will personally go ahead of you. He will be with you; he will neither fail you nor abandon you.

Deuteronomy 31:8

When you're stressed about meeting your family's needs . . .

Don't worry about these things, saying, "What will we eat? What will we drink? What will we wear?" These things dominate the thoughts of unbelievers, but your heavenly Father already knows all your needs. Seek the Kingdom of God above all else, and live righteously, and he will give you everything you need.

Matthew 6:31-33

When you need to hear something uplifting . . .

"I know the plans I have for you," says the LORD. "They are plans for good and not for disaster, to give you a future and a hope."

Jeremiah 29:11

God loved the world so much that he gave his one and only Son, so that everyone who believes in him will not perish but have eternal life. God sent his Son into the world not to judge the world, but to save the world through him.

John 3:16-17

No eye has seen, no ear has heard, and no mind has imagined what God has prepared for those who love him.

1 Corinthians 2:9

Our present troubles are small and won't last very long. Yet they produce for us a glory that vastly outweighs them and will last forever!

2 Corinthians 4:17

[John says,] "I heard a loud shout from the throne, saying, 'Look, God's home is now among his people! He will live with them, and they will be his people. God himself will be with them. He will wipe every tear from their eyes, and there will be no more death or sorrow or crying or pain. All these things are gone forever.'"

Revelation 21:3-4